I0159115

I Decide, One Day, To Make A Pizza

by Katy and Caroline Van Pelt

Blanket Press
759 Rockland Avenue, Lake Bluff, Illinois 60044
Copyright © 2011 by Katy Van Pelt
Printed in the United States
ISBN 10: 0983300011
ISBN 13: 9780983300014

For my mother, who made me my first pizza.

I decide, one day, to make a pizza - a
cheesy, bubbly, hot, delicious pizza.
I tell my family that we will be eating
at my pizzeria tonight, and then I set
to work.

It takes about two hours to make a
pizza. First you have to make the
dough, then you have to let the dough
rise, and finally you have to make and
cook the pizza.

I wash my hands and scrub them with soap, then dry them with a towel. I slip my apron over my head and tie it behind me. Now I look like a real chef.

I look around my kitchen to make sure that it is clean. A real chef always makes sure that her workspace is clean so that her food will be clean too!

I gather my cooking supplies
together…

one large bowl

one small bowl

one large wooden spoon

one small wooden spoon

some measuring cups and spoons

I get my ingredients for pizza dough...

some flour

some sugar

some yeast

some sea salt

some good olive oil.

With everything ready, it will be easy
to make a pizza!

Yeast is very important because it makes the pizza dough puffy. I need to feed the yeast so that it will help my dough to grow. Yeast likes to eat sugary water, and it likes to be warm.

I measure **one cup of water**, and I feel the water to make sure it is as warm as a nice warm bath.

I sprinkle **one tablespoon of sugar** into the water and stir it with my small wooden spoon to make warm sugary water.

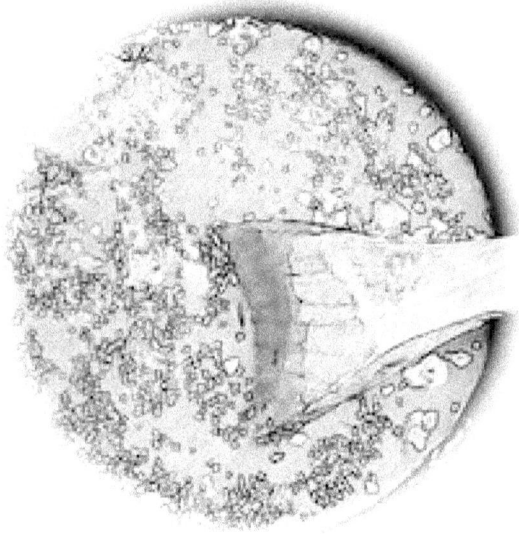

I sprinkle **one package of yeast** on top, and gently mix the yeast into the sugary water using my small wooden spoon.

I wait patiently to see if the yeast likes my sugary water.

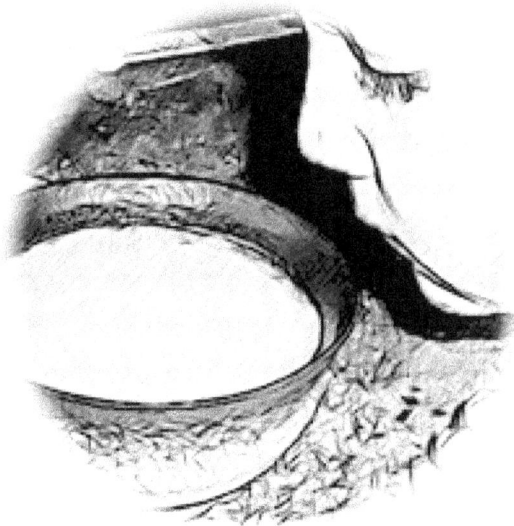

If the yeast likes my sugary water, it will grow a layer of white froth on top of the water. This takes a few minutes. The yeast begins to make little bubbles as it starts to eat the sugary water.

I can see the foam on top of the bowl.
The yeast likes my sugary water!

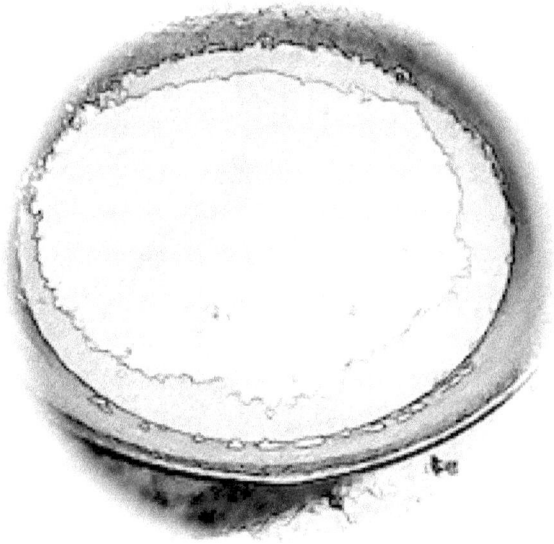

This means that it will continue to
grow and will help my dough to
become light and fluffy.

Now I am ready to mix together the flour and salt.

I carefully measure **three cups of flour**, then stir it together with **one teaspoon of sea salt**.

I make a little hole in the middle of
the flour.

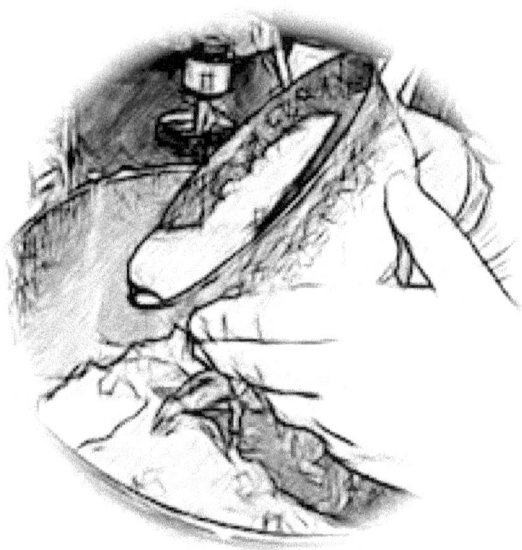

Into that hole I pour a **quarter of a
cup of olive oil** and the sugary,
watery yeast.

I stir this all together using my big
wooden spoon.

I mix and stir until all of the
ingredients have stuck together into a
rough ball.

Once the ingredients are well mixed,
it is time to knead the dough.

I sprinkle a little bit of flour on the
table. Then I pick up the ball of
dough and place it on top of the flour
on the table. I start to knead it.

To knead the dough, I press it down, then fold it over, and then press it down again.

I do this over and over again until the dough is springy and stretchy. This usually takes a few minutes.

When the dough feels ready, I pinch a bit of it between my fingers to see if it is stretchy enough.

If the dough feels sticky, I need to add a little flour. If the dough is too dry to stretch, I need to add a few drops of water. My dough does not feel too sticky or dry - it stretches perfectly!

I pour **two tablespoons of olive oil** into the bowl, roll my ball of dough in the oil and then leave it in the bowl. The oil will help the dough to stay soft.

I place a kitchen towel on top of the dough, and then I wait for the dough to grow. I try to remember how big it is, so that I will know when it has grown enough.

We have to wait for the dough to rise.
The dough needs to double in size.
This will take about one hour.

I decide to put a puzzle together while
I wait.

After one hour is up, I check my dough. It has grown very nicely, and is now a large ball of dough.

It is time to turn my dough into pizza. I wash my hands again.

I get my supplies and ingredients…

a pizza pan

a cutting board

a knife

tomato sauce

shredded mozzarella cheese

garlic, olive oil, basil and vegetables

I decide to make a small pizza for each
of us.

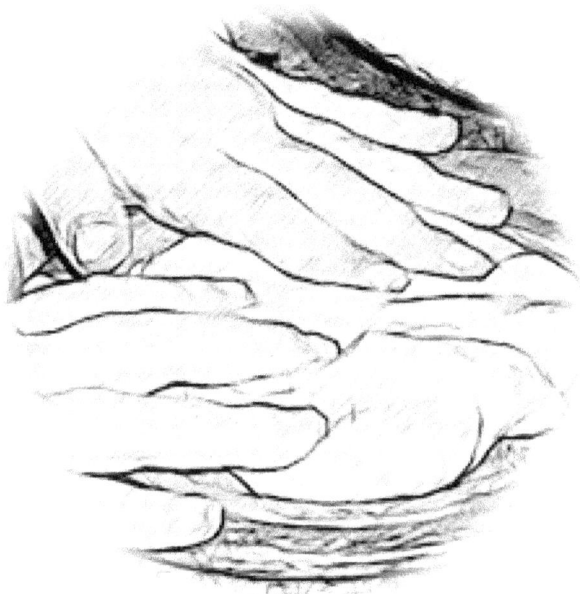

I break a piece of dough off from the
large ball and start to stretch it into a
thin circle that covers the pan.

The pizza dough looks like this when it
is stretched out on the pan.

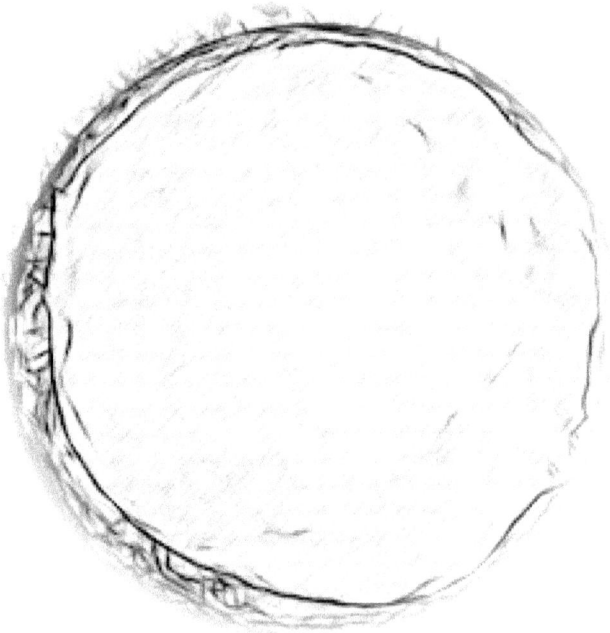

Now, like an artist with a blank
canvas, I start to think about what I
will place on top.

I spread some tomato sauce on top of
my pizzas using my small wooden
spoon.

I leave an inch around the edge of
each pizza. This will be the crust.

I sprinkle some mozzarella cheese on
top of the sauce.
I cut a tomato into small pieces, and
place those on top of the cheese.

When I use a knife, I keep my fingers
away from the sharp blade and always
make sure my mother or father is
nearby.

I tear the basil leaves into small pieces
and place those on top of the pizza.

I hold a piece of basil up so that I can
smell it.

My mother minces the garlic into little
tiny pieces, and I place them on the
very top, along with some black olives.

Finally, I brush a little bit of olive oil
around the crust.

Now, my mother turns on the oven to **500 degrees**, and I watch her place the pizzas inside. The pizzas cook for **ten minutes**, and then we begin to watch them.

Once the cheese is melted and the crusts are beginning to brown, the pizzas are done cooking.

My father takes the pizzas out of the
oven, and we let them cool for a few
minutes. They smell wonderful, and I
can't wait to eat them.

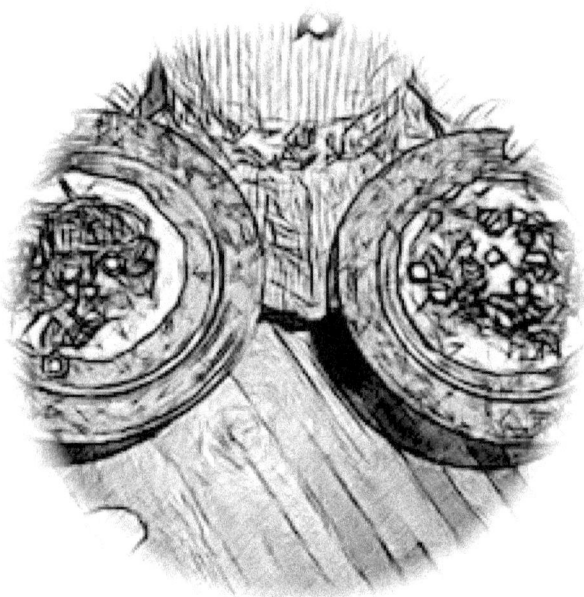

Everyone can smell the pizzas. Even
our dog comes into the kitchen hoping
for a treat.

I set the table for dinner. I think it
will be a busy night at my pizzeria!

I put a knife and a fork at each place,
and fold a napkin for each place as
well. I bring in glasses and plates, and
a pitcher of water.

Now I can sit down to enjoy my pizza.

Bon appétit!

Pizza Recipe

Ingredients:
 - 3 cups flour (plus a little more)
 - 1 package of yeast
 - 1 tablespoon sugar
 - 1 cup of warm water
 - 1 teaspoon sea salt
 - 1/4 cup of olive oil
 - toppings (sauce, cheese, vegetables)

1. Dissolve the sugar in the warm water, and sprinkle the yeast on top. Gently stir, then wait a few minutes to allow the yeast to begin growing.
2. Put three cups of flour in a large bowl, and stir in the salt. Make a hole in the middle and add the olive oil and yeast mixture. Stir.
3. Once the dough is stirred together, transfer to a table and knead it for several minutes, until it is stretchy and smooth.
4. Put the ball of dough into a bowl, coat with olive oil, and cover with a towel. Let dough double in size (about one hour).
5. Shape dough into desired shape, top with desired toppings, and bake for 10 to 15 minutes at 500 degrees F.

www.ingramcontent.com/pod-product-compliance
Lightning Source LLC
Chambersburg PA
CBHW060601030426

42337CB00019B/3583